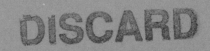

Even an Ostrich Needs a Nest

Where Birds Begin

Irene Kelly

Holiday House / New York

For Betty

The publisher would like to thank Margaret Hart, Scientific Assistant, Department of Ornithology, Division of Vertebrate Zoology, American Museum of Natural History, for checking the text and art for accuracy.

female Ruby-throated Hummingbird

Printed and Bound in Malaysia
The text typeface is Lizard.
The illustrations were done in watercolor, gouache, acrylic, and pen and ink.
www.holidayhouse.com
First Edition
1 3 5 7 9 10 8 6 4 2

Library of Congress Cataloging-in-Publication Data
Kelly, Irene.
Even an ostrich needs a nest : where birds begin / Irene Kelly. — 1st ed.
p. cm.
ISBN 978-0-8234-2102-2 (hardcover)
1. Birds—Nests—Juvenile literature. I. Title.
QL675.K45 2009
598.156'4—dc22
2007051059

What does it take to build a bird's nest?

twigs

grass

spider silk

yarn

moss

clothespins

newspaper

socks

paper clips

rubber bands

dollar bills

seeds

bark

drinking straws

bottle caps

towels, and more ...

Some birds don't build a nest at all!

Emperor penguins simply use their feet as nests.

The female lays one egg. The male balances it on top of his feet, covering it with his soft belly to keep it warm.

Potoos lay a single egg on a branch or tree stump. They sit up very tall to trick hungry predators into thinking they're twigs. Potoos can peek through the little notches in their eyelids.

The Blue-footed Booby places her warm, webbed feet over her eggs to keep them toasty.

Murres are seabirds that lay their eggs on the edges of cliffs . . . but they don't worry about them rolling off. The eggs are so pointy that they roll in a tight circle if they are nudged. Each egg has its own special pattern, so the parents can always find it.

murre egg close-up

Lots of birds build very simple nests.

Baby Bald Eagles grow up in simple nests made of layered sticks. These nests are GIGANTIC, up to ten feet wide and weighing two tons. That's as heavy as a car!

Eagle nests look sloppy, but the sticks are carefully layered to create a very strong, triangle-shaped nest. These nests are so sturdy, you and I could sit in them!

The snowy owl scrapes at the ground with her sharp talons to make a shallow bowl. She lines it with feathers and lays her eggs. Many snowy owls fly south for the winter. Some stop and stay at Logan Airport in Boston, Massachusetts, where the wide, flat runways remind them of their Arctic home.

Barn owls often use a nest abandoned in a barn or a hollow tree trunk. Sometimes they line their nests with owl feathers and mouse fur.

Most birds build a cup-shaped nest.

The American Robin weaves just such a nest out of grass, twigs, paper, and feathers. She lines the cozy nest with mud and sometimes yarn, newspaper, string . . . or maybe even dollar bills!

American Robin

A hummingbird makes the tiniest nest of all—

half as big as a Ping-Pong ball! The inside of the nest is lined with spider silk and the outside with lichen.

Costa's Hummingbird

Palm Swifts build vertical nests. The female uses saliva to glue feathers to the underside of a palm leaf. She even glues her eggs to the nest!

Palm Swift

The Yellow-rumped Thornbill
builds two nests
in one.

The top is a fake;
the little bird never uses it.
Instead, she lays her eggs
in the bottom nest.

Predators look in the top nest and think it is abandoned.
The eggs or nestlings are safe below.

Some birds, such as the American Dipper, make a cup-shaped nest with a roof. The dipper often hides its nest . . . behind a waterfall!

dipper nest made with grasses and moss

The Ovenbird hides her nest on the forest floor or underground. She uses stems, vines, and moss to create a woven cup, then she adds a roof of leaves.

The Hammerkop's nest is made of more than six thousand sticks. These nests can be six feet high and six feet wide.

feathers

snakeskin

plastic

Popcorn

trash

even pots and pans!

The outside of the Hammerkop's nest is festively decorated with

The nest has an entrance tunnel and three rooms!

The male Masked Weaver creates a hanging nest. First he tears a leaf into strips. Then he holds one end of the strip on to a branch with one foot while weaving the other end with his beak. He continues weaving the grass strips until he has a perfect nest. If the female doesn't like the nest, he will tear it apart and start over.

A Sociable Weaver's nest looks like a haystack . . . wedged in a tree!
These little birds weave dry grasses together for the nest's floor
and use twigs for the roofs. There can be one hundred chambers
in a single nest and more than two hundred birds.
The nest can last as long as one hundred years.

close-up

The weavers
enter the nest
from underneath.

Sociable Weaver

spider silk

A female tailorbird sews a leaf together to make a tiny pouch. First she wraps spider silk around a leaf to make it curl. Then the bird uses her beak to poke holes along the leaf's edge. She threads spider silk or seed fibers through the holes and teases the ends with her beak to make a ball instead of tying a knot as a human tailor would. Soft grasses and fluffy seeds line the nest.

The female Baltimore oriole weaves a hanging basket for a nest. The bird begins by wrapping grass or thin strips of bark around a branch, leaving the ends hanging.

Then she weaves grass through the hanging strands, pushing and pulling the grass strips until she has woven a pouch.

Some birds nest in a hole. The Atlantic Puffin chooses an abandoned rabbit hole or digs a burrow with its strong bill and feet. The tunnel to a puffin's nest can be eight feet long!

Grasses and feathers make a soft bed for the nestlings.

inside the burrow

Carmine Bee-eaters fly beakfirst into a cliff, creating a small dent. Then they dig until they have made an eight-foot tunnel that they line with bits of insects. This smells bad, but the odor keeps predators away.

inside the tunnel

Burrowing Owls almost never dig their own nests. Instead, they rely on the abandoned burrows of ground squirrels, foxes, skunks, prairie dogs, or armadillos. The owls pad the nests with cow or horse dung, grasses, and feathers.

Gila Woodpecker

Gila Woodpeckers peck holes in saguaro cacti and nest inside. Sometimes a tiny female Elf Owl appears carrying a live Western Blind Snake! The woodpecker lets the owl and the snake move into the cactus. Why? Because the snake eats the annoying bugs in the nest. The owl and the woodpecker take turns hunting and roosting, keeping all the chicks safe.

Elf Owl

Western Blind Snake

Every year, Pileated woodpeckers hammer new holes in trees with their strong beaks. They can peck a tree twenty times per SECOND.

The female hornbill squeezes herself into a hole in a tree.
Then the pair of hornbills seals the hole with their
droppings and mud until the female is walled inside.
The male feeds her through a small opening
for the next four months,
while she lays and hatches her
eggs inside her snug chamber.
She won't break the barrier until
the chicks are two weeks old.

female hornbill on nest

Tundra swans also nest on simple mounds. A pair will spend a week or two piling up vegetation—often on top of a muskrat or beaver lodge. The female makes a hollow in the mound by pressing down with her body. The pair will use this nest year after year.

Wandering Albatrosses build mounds of mud and vegetation, usually on cliffs from which they can easily take off. A single egg is laid in November, hatching two months later. The chick stays in the nest for nine months.

For the Australian Brush-turkey, a HUGE pile of leaves and soil makes an excellent nest. As the leaves rot, they create heat, which incubates the eggs. The female lays one egg every other day in small holes in the nest until about twenty-four eggs have been laid.

After fifty days the chicks hatch. They dig their way out and run into the brush, where they are on their own.

The Brush-turkey's nest can be thirteen feet across and four feet high!

A pair of Common Loons uses grasses, weeds, sticks, and water plants to create their nest on the edge of a lake.

The male jacana makes a floating nest from plants. After the female lays her eggs, she leaves all the incubating to the male.

If the jacana's nest sinks, the male will tuck the eggs under his wings and carry them to a new site.

The Horned Coot builds an entire island before starting on a nest! The male and female drop one stone after another into a shallow part of a lake. Eventually, the rock pile reaches the water's surface. A nest of water plants is built on top of the tiny island. This nest can weigh more than an elephant!

There can be one thousand birds in just one colony!

Some birds make mud nests.

Cliff swallows usually construct their mud homes on buildings, bridges, and other man-made structures. Each nest is made up of at least one thousand mud pellets that the tiny birds carry in their beaks.

The Black-browed Albatross mixes mud with seaweed, grasses, and droppings to create a snug bowl nest.

Flamingo mud nests can be one foot high to protect the eggs from floods.

The birds use their bills to pull mud toward their feet until they have created a mound. The female will lay a single egg.

Some birds are cheaters.

They lay their eggs in other birds' nests. The female cuckoo watches a Reed Warbler build her nest. When the nest is finished, the cuckoo darts over and throws one of the warbler's eggs out! In a flash, the cuckoo lays her own egg in the nest, leaving the warbler to incubate and take care of the fast-growing hatchling.

Reed Warbler (adult)

cuckoo (chick)

Cowbirds cheat too. They often lay their eggs in Dickcissels' nests. Although the cowbird eggs are much larger, the Dickcissels rarely notice because the colors and patterns usually match.

cowbird egg in a Dickcissel's nest

cowbird

Dickcissel

Male bowerbirds create an enclosure called a bower. The Satin Bowerbird weaves hundreds of twigs together, making walls with an opening facing north. He collects and arranges objects in front of the opening. Then the bird grasps a twig or leaf in his beak, dips it in berry juice, and paints the walls of the bower! The bower is made to dazzle a female. After the pair has mated, the female will fly away and build a simple nest nearby.

drinking straws

ribbons

clothespins

parrot feathers

pen caps

toothbrushes

buttons

bottle caps

snail shells

The satin Bowerbird loves to use blue objects as decorations for his bower. Sometimes he makes a border out of snail shells.

female

The male Vogelkop Bowerbird spends
months creating the fanciest bower of all.
He weaves sticks around a young tree, shaping a small hut.
The bower has an arched doorway—something
an architect would need math to build!
The small bird lays out a moss
carpet on which he shows off his
colorful treasures in neat piles.

leaves

flowers

ginger berries

So what does it take to build a bird's nest?
There are different answers for different kinds of birds.
But whether simple or fancy, every species finds a way
to create a cozy nest that is the perfect home
for raising a family.

feathers

male Vogelkop

beetle shells

Going on a bird safari?

Here's where you'll find
the birds in this book:

1. American Dipper – western Alaska to Panama, mountainous regions of South America

2. American Robin – Alaska, Canada to southern Mexico

3. Atlantic Puffin – coastal and sea islands: southern Greenland, Iceland, Newfoundland, British Isles

4. Australian Brush-turkey – eastern Australia

5. Bald Eagle – Alaska, Canada to southern United States

6. Baltimore Oriole – Canada, eastern and central United States; winters in American tropics

7. Barn Owl – nearly worldwide in tropical and temperate areas

8. Black-browed Albatross – southern Australia, Falkland Islands

9. Blue-footed Booby – Gulf of California to Peru

10. Burrowing Owl – southwestern Canada, western Florida to southern Argentina

11. Carmine Bee-eater – Africa

12. Cliff Swallow – Alaska, Canada, Mexico; winters in Brazil, Argentina, Chile

13. Common Loon – Alaska, Canada, northern United States, Greenland, Iceland; winters in coastal Florida, northern Mexico, western Europe

14. Costa's Hummingbird – Arizona, California

15. Cowbird – southern Canada to northern Mexico; winters occasionally in Mexico

16. Cuckoo – Europe, western Asia; winters in Africa

17. Dickcissel – southern Ontario, interior of United States between Rockies and Appalachian mountains; winters in Mexico to South America

18. Elf Owl – southwestern United States and Mexico

19. Emperor Penguin – Antarctic

20. Flamingo – West Indies, Yucatán, Galápagos Islands, Florida coast

21. Gila Woodpecker – southeastern California, southern Nevada, Arizona, New Mexico

22. Hammerkop – southern and central Africa, the Arabian Peninsula, Madagascar

23. Hornbill – Asia, India to Thailand and south to Sumatra

24. Horned Coot – South America

25. Jacana – central and South America, Africa, India, Australia, Asia

26. Masked Weaver – South Africa, Angola, Democratic Republic of the Congo, Zambia, Tanzania

27. Murre – northern Atlantic Ocean, northern Pacific Ocean, Arctic islands

28. Ovenbird – southern Canada, United States east of Rockies; winters in southeastern United States to northern South America

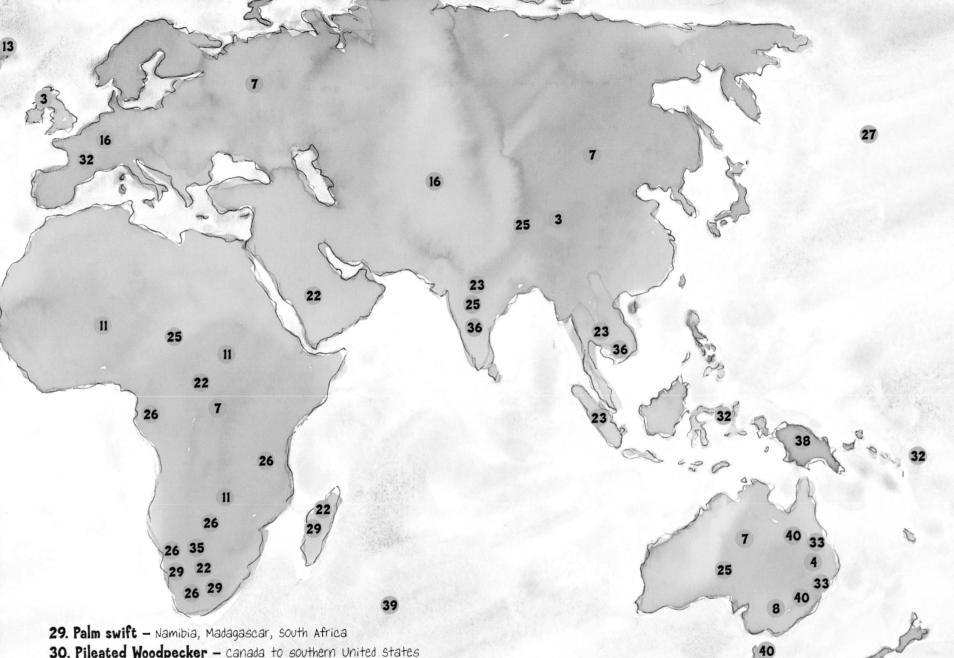

29. Palm swift – Namibia, Madagascar, South Africa

30. Pileated Woodpecker – Canada to southern United states

31. Potoo – central and south America from Mexico to Uruguay, Hispaniola, Jamaica

32. Reed Warbler – Europe through Australasia, tropical Pacific

33. Satin Bowerbird – eastern and southeastern coast of Australia

34. Snowy Owl – Arctic; winters south into United states

35. Sociable Weaver – Kalahari region of southern Africa

36. Tailorbird – Southeast Asia, India

37. Tundra Swan – North America

38. Vogelkop Bowerbird – New Guinea

39. Wandering Albatross – between Antarctica and Tropic of Capricorn

40. Yellow-rumped Thornbill – eastern and southeastern Australia, including Tasmania

YOU CAN HELP!

There are birds in every corner of the world. You can help the birds in your neighborhood build their nests by gathering together some of their favorite nesting materials:

twigs

dried leaves

bits of yarn or string

dog or cat fur

feathers

bits of aluminum foil

small strips of cloth

Stuff the fluffy nesting materials into a mesh bag (an old onion bag is perfect) and tie it onto a tree branch.

Make piles of twigs, leaves, and foil on the ground.

Watch the birds pull the materials through the holes in the bag! Go on a nest safari; you may spot a familiar scrap of cloth or yarn woven into a bird's nest.